THE
SPACE
CREATIVITY
BOOK

Budding astronauts sign up
here for a voyage to the
edge of our galaxy.

There's lots to draw, puzzles and
games to play, and stickers to take
on your adventure!

WHAT'S INSIDE THIS BOOK?

THIS BOOK IS ALL YOURS!

This book about space has lots of space for you too. You can write, draw, colour and fill up pages using your own imagination.

THINGS TO MAKE AND BAKE

Build your own solar system on page 17 or mix up some Alien Bug Juice on page 28. Snack on Meteorite Bites on page 51, make an alien mask on page 53 or craft your own souvenir plaque on page 70. There's tonnes to do, including pages of special space paper to get creative with!

SUPER STICKERS

There are loads of cool stickers waiting for you at the back of this book along with two huge fold-out intergalactic scenes. You can use your stickers here, on pages 66, 72, 76 or anywhere you like on Earth or in outer space.

PUZZLES AND GAMES

With picture puzzles, mazes, spot-the-differences, memory games, quizzes and a Race to Mars board game on page 20, there's no reason to get bored on your long journeys between the planets.

This is a Carlton book.
Text, design and illustration © Carlton Books 2013, 2019

This edition published in 2019 by Carlton Books Limited, an imprint of the Carlton Publishing Group, 20 Mortimer Street, London, W1T 3JW.

A catalogue record for this book is available from the British Library.

10 9 8 7 6 5 4
ISBN: 978-1-78312-464-0
Printed and bound in China

AUTHOR: William Potter

ILLUSTRATIONS:
Andrea Castellani
Anna Stiles

PICTURE CREDITS

The publishers would like to thank the following sources for their kind permission to reproduce the pictures in this book.

Key: T: Top, B: bottom, L: Left, R: Right, C: Centre

NASA: 1, 5, 13t, 14t, 27, 47, all postcards (p73)
Stock.XCHNG: 28
Thinkstockphotos.co.uk: 11, 12, 13b, 14b, 31

Every effort has been made to acknowledge correctly and contact the source and/or copyright holder of each picture and Carlton Books Limited apologises for any unintentional errors or omissions, which will be corrected in future editions of this book.

CALLING ALL ASTRONAUTS!

Hi. Astronaut Sam here. Happy to have you aboard. Before take-off I need to find out a few things about you.

Complete this simple space profile by ticking your answers.

1. What is your home planet?
   ○ Earth
   ○ Mars
   ○ Red Giant 572 A
   ○ Alien world

2. How far have you been from home?
   ○ A few miles
   ○ To another country
   ○ To the Moon
   ○ Over a light year* away
   * That's 5,878,625 million miles

3. What's the most time you have spent away from your family?
   ○ One to two days
   ○ A week
   ○ A year
   ○ 100 years or more

4. How many aliens have you met?
   ○ None
   ○ One
   ○ Several
   ○ Not sure – hard to tell

5. What skills can you bring to outer space? (Tick as many as you like)
   ○ I can draw
   ○ I'm good at spotting
   ○ I like adventure
   ○ I don't get scared easily
   ○ I can read maps
   ○ I'm tidy (no space junk!)
   ○ I like making friends (even with aliens)

THE ASTRO AGENCY

Stick in or draw a picture of yourself for your Astro Agency pass photo

TOP-SECRET SPACE MISSION!

Time to choose your mission. It's going to be the adventure of a lifetime, but you'll be away from Earth for a very long time, and calls home are extremely expensive. Make sure you pack all you need. Are you ready?

- CHOOSE YOUR SPACESHIP -

- CHOOSE YOUR MISSION -

☐ Exploring planets

☐ Protecting the space lanes

☐ Meeting aliens

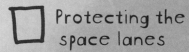
PATROL

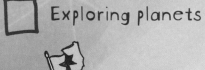

MAKE SURE YOU PACK THE FOLLOWING

☐ Star map

☐ Camera

☐ Toothbrush

☐ Journal

CHOOSE ONE LUXURY ITEM TO BRING ALONG

☐ Soft toy

☐ Guitar

☐ Computer game

OR WRITE YOUR OWN HERE

....

....

WHAT DO YOU WANT TO SEE?
Choose as many as you like

THE MOON ☐

VENUS ☐

MARS ☐

ASTEROID BELT ☐

JUPITER ☐

SATURN ☐

STATION GAMMA ALPHA ☐

COMET ☐

ALIEN WORLD ☐

BLACK HOLE ☐

SUPERNOVA ☐

SPACE NEEDS YOU!

Answer the questions to find out what top job you can expect in outer space.

START

What do you like to do on holiday?

MAKE PLANS FOR EVERY DAY

GO BEACH-COMBING

MAKE NEW FRIENDS

Have you ever been left in charge of things?

Do you like to spend a lot of time on your own?

YES

NO

NO

Are you good with gadgets?

YES

Do your relatives and friends understand you?

YES

NO

When things go wrong, what do you do?

ASK FOR HELP

Are you good at taking careful notes?

NO

YES

Are you good with words?

PUT THINGS RIGHT

NO

YES

NO

Do you like to be in control?

NO

Do you like to poke your nose into things?

NO

Do you mind your friends' strange habits?

YES

YES

YES

NO

STARSHIP CAPTAIN
With your leadership skills and ambition, you'll make a fine starship captain one day.

PLANET EXPLORER
Millions of planets out there need a skilful, careful person like you to investigate them.

ALIEN AMBASSADOR
We need you to make friends with our interstellar neighbours and learn about their alien ways.

ROCKET LAUNCH

To get up into space, you'll need a rocket.
Draw your own in this step-by-step guide.

1.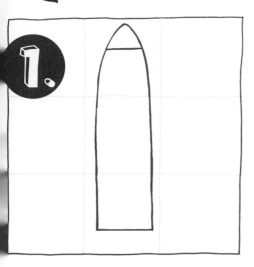

Draw the main body of your rocket with a cone at the top.

2.

Add two lines halfway down the rocket and wings at the bottom.

3.

Draw two triangular thrusters at the bottom of the rocket. Add stripes to the middle section.

4.

3-2-1 blast off!
Draw flames and smoke coming from the engines.

DID YOU KNOW?
Your rocket will need to reach a speed of 7 miles per second to leave Earth. That speed would get you from London to New York in less than ten minutes!

SUIT UP!

Copy the details from the left-hand side to finish your spacesuit. Then add your mission badge to the pocket.

HELMET LIGHT AND CAMERA
Space is dark. You'll need lights and a camera to record your discoveries.

VISOR
Your helmet's tinted visor is lined with gold for extra protection against the Sun's bright rays.

LIFE SUPPORT
You'll need to carry your own air supply into space, of course, plus cooling water and a radio to keep you in contact with the ship.

WATER POUCH
When you're thirsty in space, you can drink through a tube from a water pouch near your chest.

LAYERS
There are 14 layers to your spacesuit, to protect you from heat, cold, fire and impacts. It takes a long time to get in and out of it!

THRUSTERS
These small rockets help you get back to your ship if you start floating away in space.

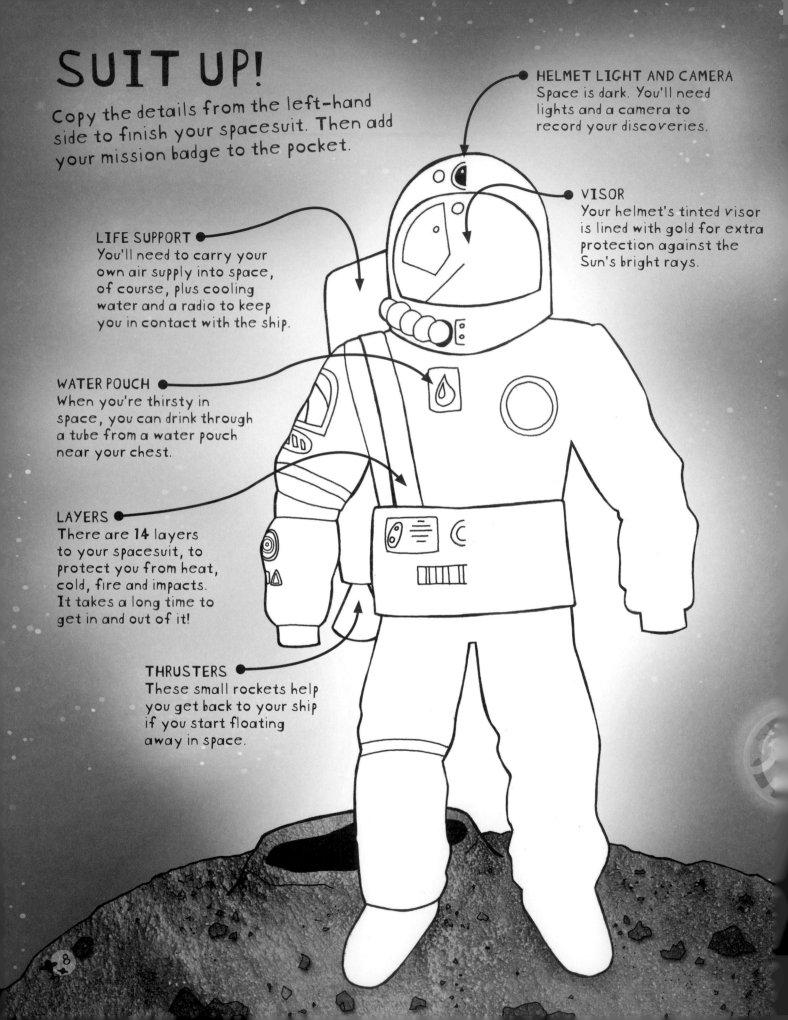

STAR MAP

Follow the directions across this map of an alien solar system. Where will you end up?

	A	B	C	D	E	F	G	H	I	J	K	L	M	N	
1		ZOG													1
2							MAGNIFICA					WHOPPA			2
3															3
4															4
5															5
6							MOONLET								6
7															7
8	SPACE STATION												YIS		8
9					ALFIRIS										9
10															10
	A	B	C	D	E	F	G	H	I	J	K	L	M	N	

DIRECTIONS!

Start at Zog, square B2.
Zoom down four squares.
Go right three squares towards the moonlet.
Move two squares towards Alfiris.
Go right four squares.
Hop one square up.
Rush four squares past the asteroids.
Rocket four squares up.

COLOUR IN THE PLANETS

WHERE ARE YOU NOW? ....

Turn to page 80 for the answer.

Amazing things to do with your SPACE PAPER

Here are four great things you can do with the SPACE PAPER on pages 12 and 13.

1. Use the paper to decorate your own astronaut-training manual and space journal.

2. Draw shapes of planets and spaceships on the back of your space paper, then cut them out. Find a sheet of black paper and add spots of white paint for stars. Then glue your space-paper planets and rockets on top for your own space mural.

3. Cut out photos of yourself and friends to place on top of the backgrounds for your own outer-space adventures.

4. Cut out the pictures and glue them on to large plain sheets to make wrapping paper.

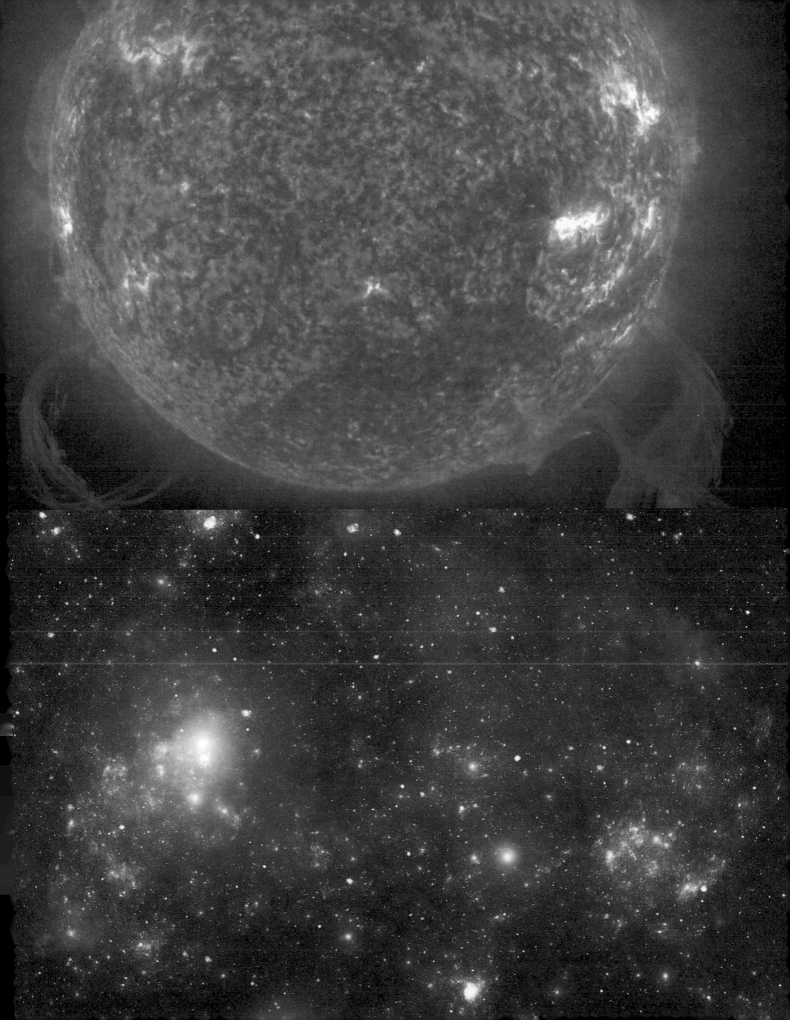

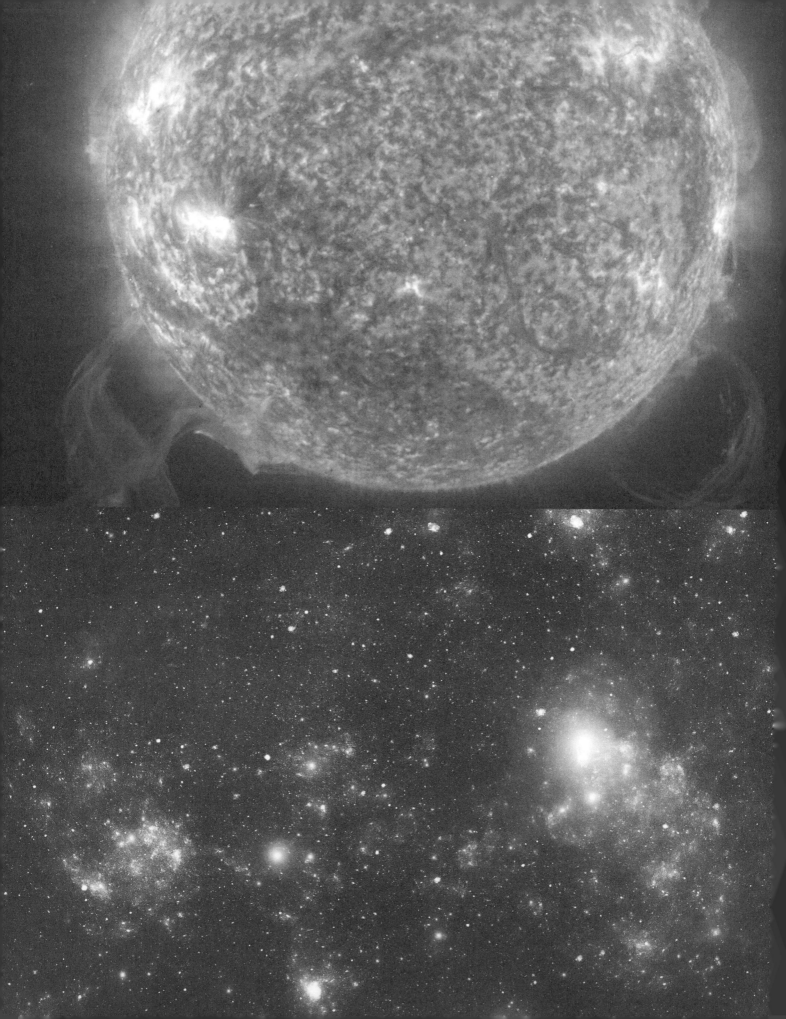

BIG BANG BY NUMBERS

Most scientists agree that the universe began more than 13 billion years ago, with one incredible event — THE BIG BANG!

Colour in the beginning of space and time following the colour key.

1. GREEN
2. YELLOW
3. ORANGE
4. RED
5. PURPLE
6. BLUE

DID YOU KNOW?
The Big Bang was seriously hot. At the first tiny fraction of a second of its beginning, it is reckoned to have been over 10,000,000,000,000,000,000,000,000,000,000°C!

TOUCHDOWN!

Spot the **10** differences between these two pictures of the first Moon landing.

 Turn to page 80 for the answer.

The first successful mission to land people on the moon and bring them safely home was Apollo 11 in July 1969. U.S. astronauts Neil Armstrong and Edwin 'Buzz' Aldrin were the first people to walk on the lunar surface.

SOLAR SYSTEM

Put together your own mobile with the planets rotating around the Sun.

URANUS

SIZE: 63 x Earth

DAY: 17 hours

DISTANCE FROM SUN:
1.8 billion miles

SURFACE TEMPERATURE:
−214°C

MERCURY

SIZE: 0.06 x Earth

DAY: 59 Earth days

DISTANCE FROM SUN:
36 million miles

SURFACE TEMPERATURE:
−180 to 430°C

THE SUN

SIZE:
1.3 million x Earth

DAY:
34 Earth days

SURFACE TEMPERATURE:
5,500°C

JUPITER

SIZE: 1,321 x Earth

DAY: 10 hours

DISTANCE FROM SUN:
484 million miles

SURFACE TEMPERATURE:
−110°C

EARTH

SIZE: 1,083 billion cubic km

DAY: 24 hours

DISTANCE FROM SUN:
93 million miles

SURFACE TEMPERATURE:
Average 15°C

VENUS

SIZE: 0.8 x Earth

DAY: 243 Earth days

DISTANCE FROM SUN:
67 million miles

SURFACE TEMPERATURE:
464°C

MARS

SIZE: 0.15 x Earth

DAY: 25 hours

DISTANCE FROM SUN:
142 million miles

SURFACE TEMPERATURE:
−125 to 25°C

NEPTUNE

SIZE: 58 x Earth

DAY: 16 hours

DISTANCE FROM SUN: 2.8 billion miles

SURFACE TEMPERATURE: −220°C

SATURN

SIZE: 764 x Earth

DAY: 11 hours

DISTANCE FROM SUN:
888 million miles

SURFACE TEMPERATURE:
−140°C

HOW TO MAKE YOUR PLANET MOBILE

YOU WILL NEED:

Paper plate · Pencil · Modelling clay · Scissors · String · Sticky tape

1. Find the centre of your paper plate and carefully push a pencil through the middle into modelling clay to make a hole. This is where the Sun will hang from.

2. Use the pencil and clay to make another eight holes spaced around the plate. Four should be close to the middle, four near the edge. These will be your planets' orbits around the Sun.

3. Carefully cut out your planets and the Sun, and tape a 15cm length of string to the back of each one.

4. Thread the other end of each string through a hole in the plate in this order from the centre: Sun, Mercury, Venus, Earth, Mars, Jupiter, Saturn, Uranus, Neptune.

5. Now stick a length of string to the top of your paper plate to hang up your mobile.

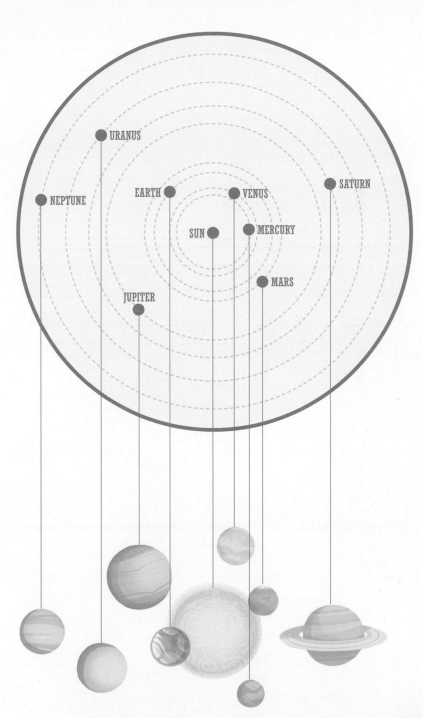

URANUS

NEPTUNE

EARTH

VENUS

SATURN

SUN

MERCURY

MARS

JUPITER

RACE TO THE RED PLANET
Who will reach Mars first?

HOW TO PLAY

🛸 Find a die and something you can use for counters.

🪐 Place your counters on START and take it in turns to roll the die. The first one to roll a 6 goes first.

🧠 MOVE FORWARD the number of squares shown on the die then follow the instructions written on the squares.

🧑 The first person to reach Mars is the WINNER!

24 FOLLOW THE COMET TO SEE WHERE IT LEADS.

5 COMPUTER MALFUNCTION. MISS A GO TO MAKE REPAIRS.

4

23

6 TEST SOME POWERFUL NEW ION ENGINES. DOUBLE YOUR MOVE.

3 BONK! YOU HIT SOME SPACE JUNK. GO BACK TWO SPACES.

7

2 ROCKET BOOSTERS FIRE. ROLL AGAIN.

8 EMERGENCY CALL. ZOOM FORWARD THREE SPACES.

9 VISIT MOONBASE FOR LUNCH. MISS A TURN.

START

BLAST OFF!

SPACE FOOD

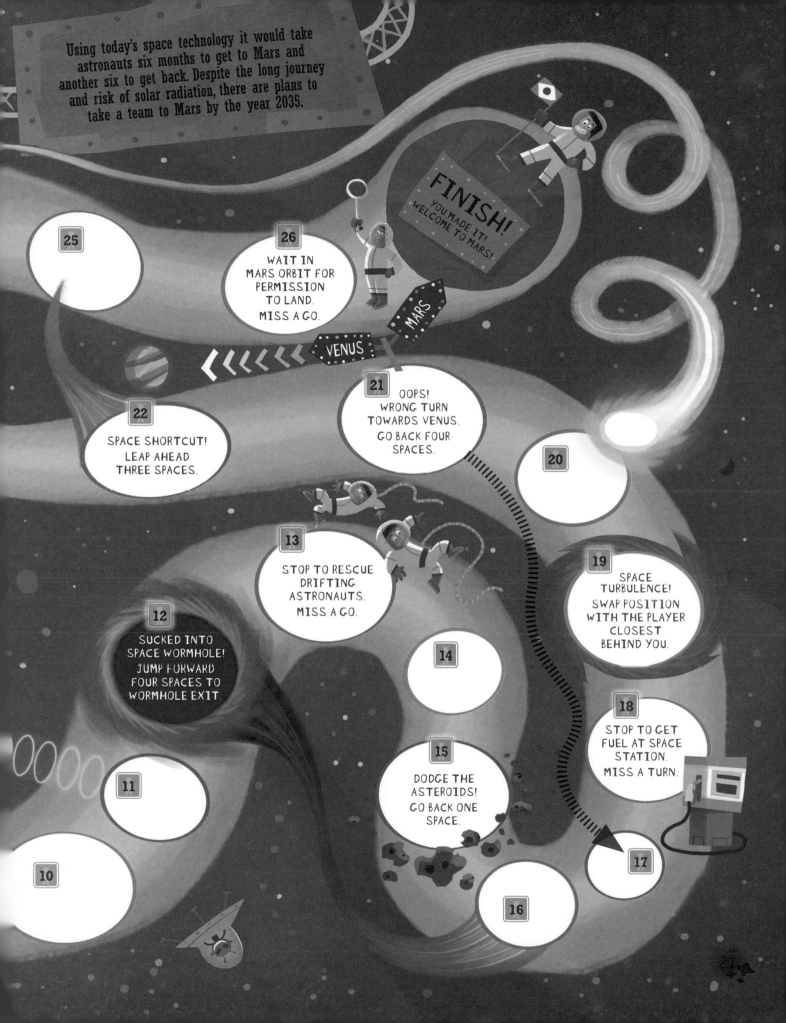

STARGAZER

For thousands of years, people have found their way across the sky by giving names to groups of stars called constellations.

Here are just a few.

PERSEUS
Brave Perseus defeated the monstrous snake-headed Medusa whose stare turned people to stone. He carries her head in one hand and a sword in the other.

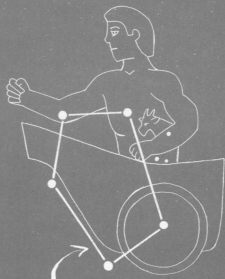

AURIGA
Legend says that Auriga invented the chariot. He rides it across the night sky, carrying a young goat under his arm.

CASSIOPEIA
Cassiopeia was a queen who got in trouble with the gods for boasting that she was one of the most beautiful women in the world.

ORION
Orion, the son of the sea god Poseidon, was a great hunter but a bit of a bighead. Despite all his fighting skills, he was killed by a tiny scorpion.

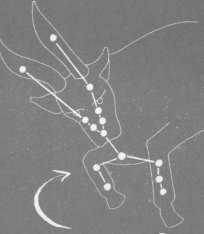

TAURUS
Taurus the bull is one of the 12 signs of the zodiac in the night sky. In Greek myth, the king of the gods, Zeus, disguised himself as a bull.

When you're travelling in outer space, you'll see different stars to the ones that are visible from Earth.

Draw some of the new constellations that you think you might find.

PASSPORT TO THE PLANETS

There are lots of incredible sights to see on your way through the solar system.

Follow the tangled paths to match the amazing views with each planet.

MERCURY

VENUS

MARS

PLANET-SIZED STORM
Welcome to the solar system's biggest planet. The big red spot in its cloudy atmosphere is a super-massive hurricane that's been raging for over 300 years. The storm is so big, you could fit two Earths inside it.

BIGGEST MOUNTAIN
At 16 miles tall, the extinct volcano Olympus Mons is about two-and-a-half times higher than Earth's highest mountain, Everest. In fact, it's the biggest mountain in the whole solar system!

DIAMOND RAIN
This huge planet of gas has an atmosphere of poisonous methane, and winds that blow as fast as 1,340 miles per hour. The air pressure is so great that the gases may be squeezed into falling diamonds!

Turn to page 80 for the answer.

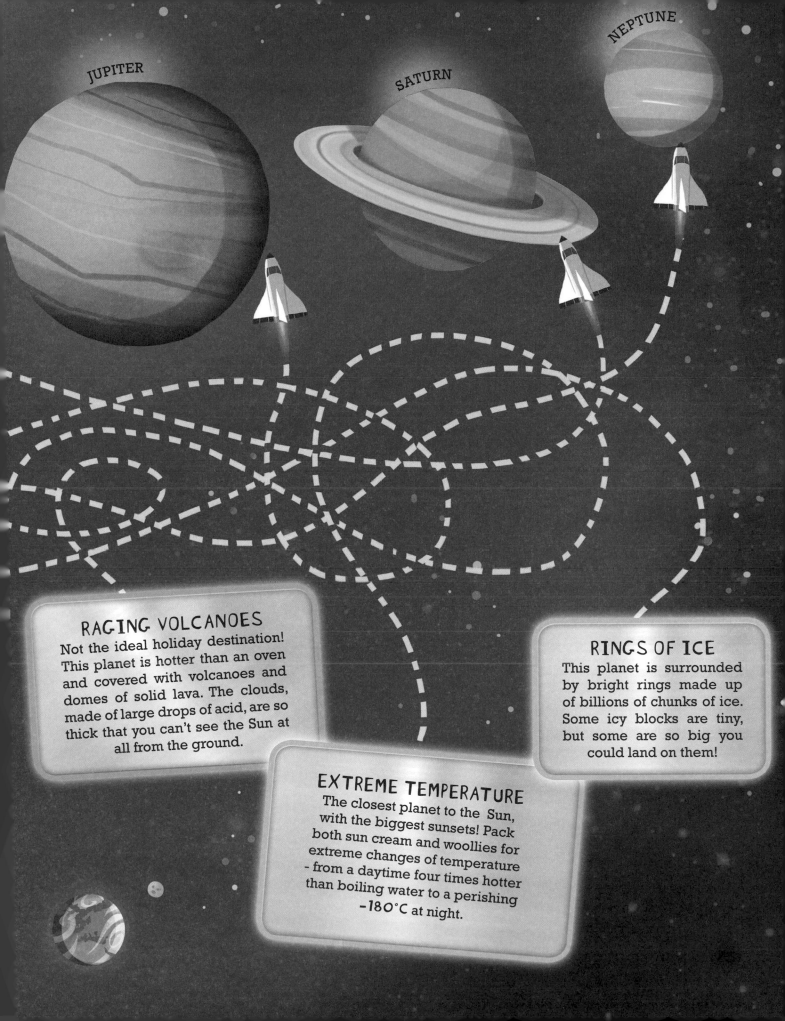

JUPITER

SATURN

NEPTUNE

RAGING VOLCANOES
Not the ideal holiday destination!
This planet is hotter than an oven
and covered with volcanoes and
domes of solid lava. The clouds,
made of large drops of acid, are so
thick that you can't see the Sun at
all from the ground.

EXTREME TEMPERATURE
The closest planet to the Sun,
with the biggest sunsets! Pack
both sun cream and woollies for
extreme changes of temperature
- from a daytime four times hotter
than boiling water to a perishing
-180°C at night.

RINGS OF ICE
This planet is surrounded
by bright rings made up
of billions of chunks of ice.
Some icy blocks are tiny,
but some are so big you
could land on them!

GO ROVER!

Copy each square of this drawing of the Mars Curiosity rover in the right order in the grid opposite.

3C

2A

1D

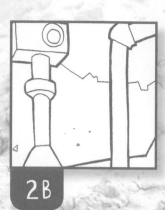
2B

1A

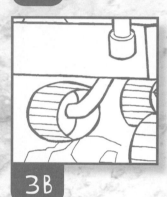
3B

1C

4D

2D

4A

3D

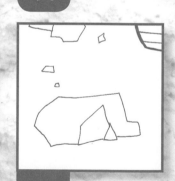
4B

2C

1B

4C

3A

DID YOU KNOW?
NASA's Curiosity Rover is a robotic, car-sized laboratory that successfully landed on the surface of Mars in August 2012. It is digging, drilling and testing rocks to look for evidence that Mars may have once supported life or could even still host it now.

ALIEN BUG JUICE

Spaceflight can be long and dull at times. Perk things up with this alien bug juice, perfect for an interplanetary party with your astrobuddies.

INGREDIENTS
(makes two drinks)

1 cup of apple juice
2 teaspoons of runny honey
ice
2 cups of sparkling water
mint leaves
small cubes of peeled cucumber

DIRECTIONS

1. Divide the apple juice between two tall glasses and stir a teaspoon of honey into each.

2. Top up each glass with ice and sparking water.

3. Decorate with mint leaves and cubes of cucumber for alien bugs.

WEIGHTLESS

Here's a nice, peaceful view of life in space. But a moment later, someone turns off the artificial gravity!

Finish the second picture to show the food, drinks, pens, pads and tools floating around in the spacecraft, then fill in the word balloons with what you think the astronauts are saying.

DESIGN A SPACE PROBE

Can you build your own space probe
for studying the stars? Use the
parts suggested, if you like, then
launch it into space!

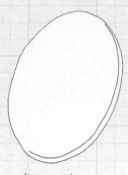

thermal
shield

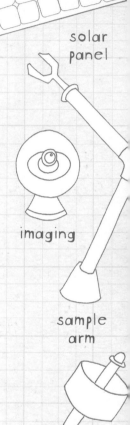

solar
panel

imaging

sample
arm

star tracker

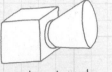

asteroid
detector

spectrometer

landing
gear

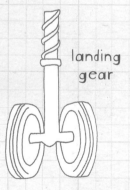

thermo-generator

antenna

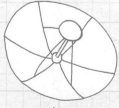

camera

vacuum gauge

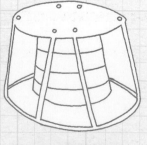

sample
capsule

engine

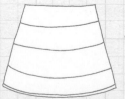

electronics

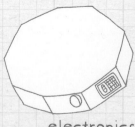

aliens?

SEEING THINGS

What do you think your space probe will discover?
Draw some ideas in the space below...

comet

MARS MISSION

You've arrived at Mars base! Grab your pencils to finish off the scene.

Add a rocket leaving Mars.

Draw a space station in orbit.

Add a planet sticker.

Draw a Mars rover.

Build a robot.

32

Add a galaxy.

Draw a radar dish.

Add details to the Mars Astronaut Base.

Draw a spaceship.

SPACE MUSEUM HEIST

Call the space rangers! There's been a theft at the Interplanetary Space Museum. Help the museum by drawing the missing exhibits back in place. Look at the signs for help.

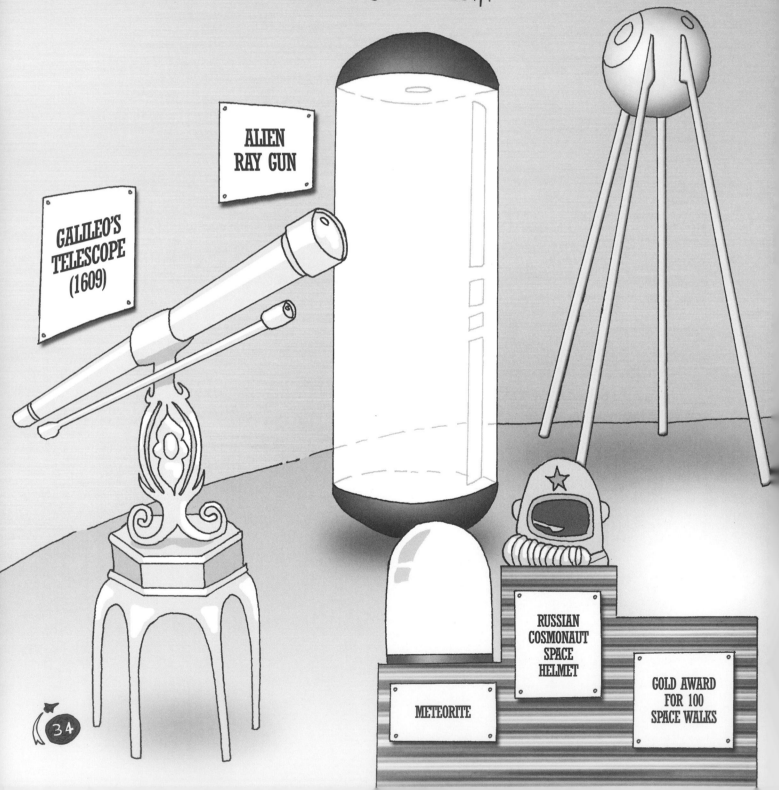

SPUTNIK 1
EARTH'S FIRST ARTIFICIAL SATELLITE
(1957)

ALIEN RAY GUN

GALILEO'S TELESCOPE
(1609)

RUSSIAN COSMONAUT SPACE HELMET

METEORITE

GOLD AWARD FOR 100 SPACE WALKS

34

ASTEROID ALERT!

Your mission has reached the deadly asteroid belt between Mars and Jupiter. Can you make your way through the space rocks to safety?

START

FINISH

Turn to page 80 for the answer.

WHAT CAN YOU SEE?

Take a look through the telescope.

HELP

MEMORY QUEST

Now try to draw all of the things you saw on the last page!

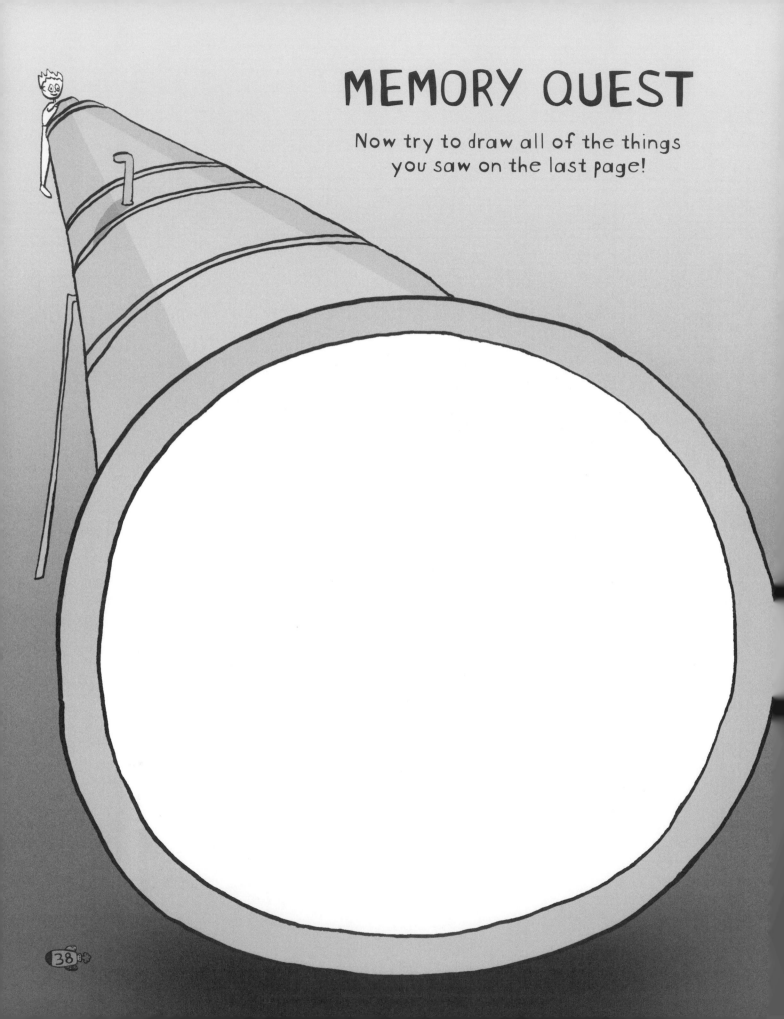

ONCE UPON A TIME IN OUTER SPACE...

Make up your own space story using some
of the pictures and words provided.

MY ROCKET BLASTED OFF.
I WAS ON A MISSION TO...

EARTH WAS SAVED! THE END.

PICTURES

WORDS

SPACESHIP
HYPERSPEED
BLACK HOLE
ALIEN INVASION
ASTEROIDS
SPACE STATION
ZAPPED
STRANGE
MONSTER
EXPLOSION

STAR WRECKS

Look at all the starships in the wrecking yard. Can you match up the 10 pairs and find one left over?

40

Write the matching pairs in these boxes

WRITE THE ODD ONE OUT HERE

K

L

M

O

N

R

P

Q

U

T

S

Turn to page 80 for the answer.

SPACE PIRATES!

Your mission of peace has been attacked by space pirates wanting to steal your supplies.

The valiant starship captain (you!)

42

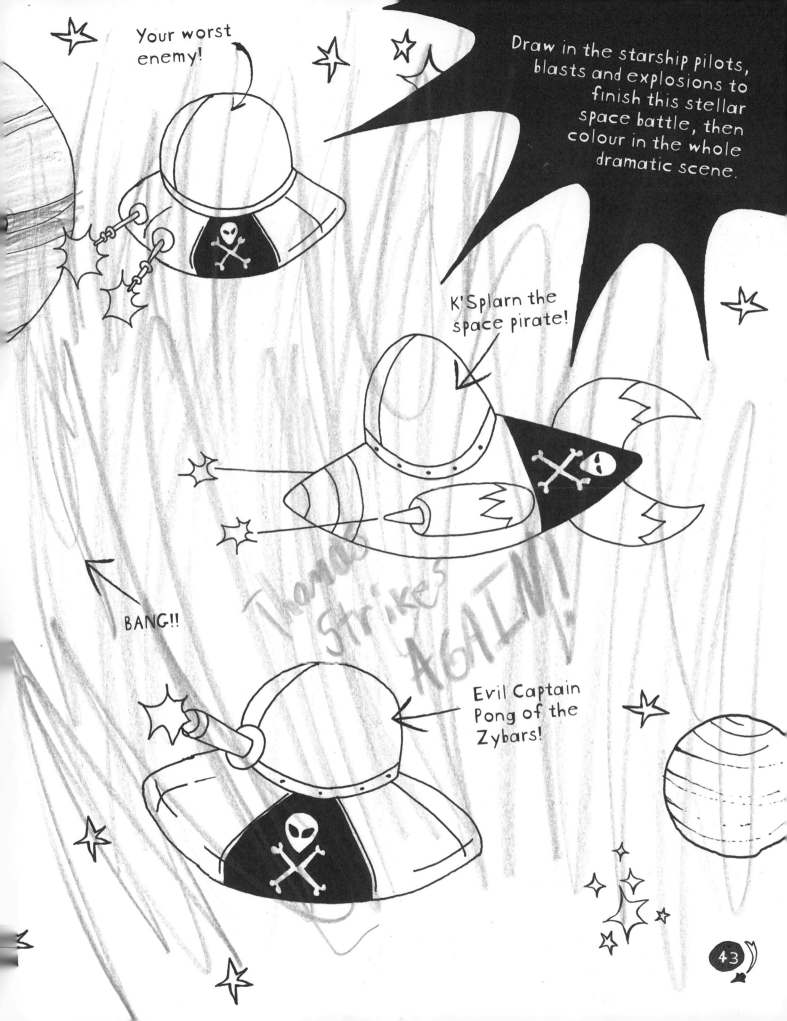

CYBORG CREW

Meet Cogs. He's a cyborg — a half-robot/half-human member of your crew.

Draw the robot parts where you think they belong to finish off his body.

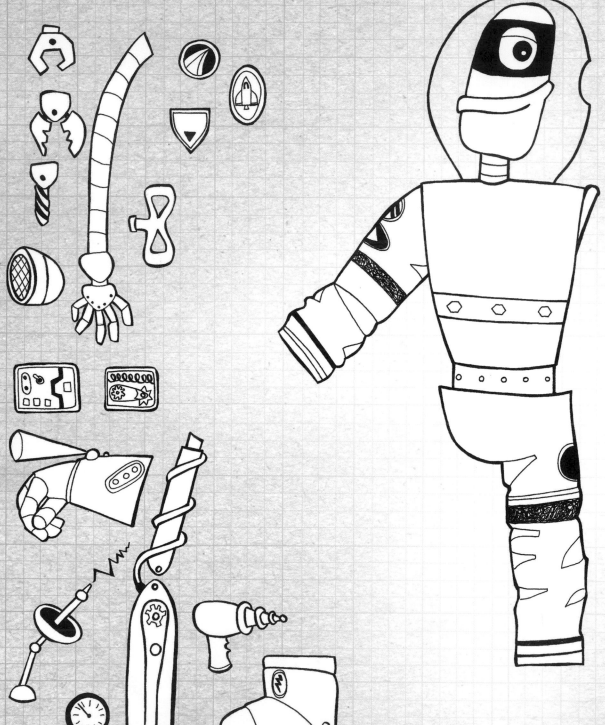

44

DEEP SPACE DOOR HANGERS

It's been a busy spaceflight so far. Time for a snooze. Make sure you're not disturbed by carefully cutting out these handy door hangers.

HOW TO MAKE YOUR DOOR HANGERS

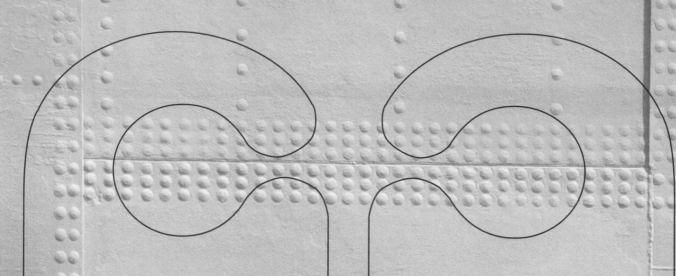

1. Ask a grown up to help you **CUT OUT** the two door hanger shapes.

2. **STICK** the two shapes back-to-back to make one hanger.

3. **HANG** it on your bedroom door, showing whichever side you want!

STRETCH AND SQUASH

What would people look like if they lived in stronger or weaker gravity?

WHAT IS GRAVITY?

Gravity is the force that makes things fall to the ground and stops us floating away from Earth. On some huge planets, like Jupiter, gravity is stronger than on Earth, which would make you feel almost three times heavier. On Mars, it's lighter, so we could leap three times as high into the sky.

EARTH

MARS

Copy the astronaut as a squashed, heavier person on Jupiter and as a tall, lighter person on Mars, with much less gravity.

JUPITER

RING AROUND SATURN

Can you guide your spaceship safely through the maze?

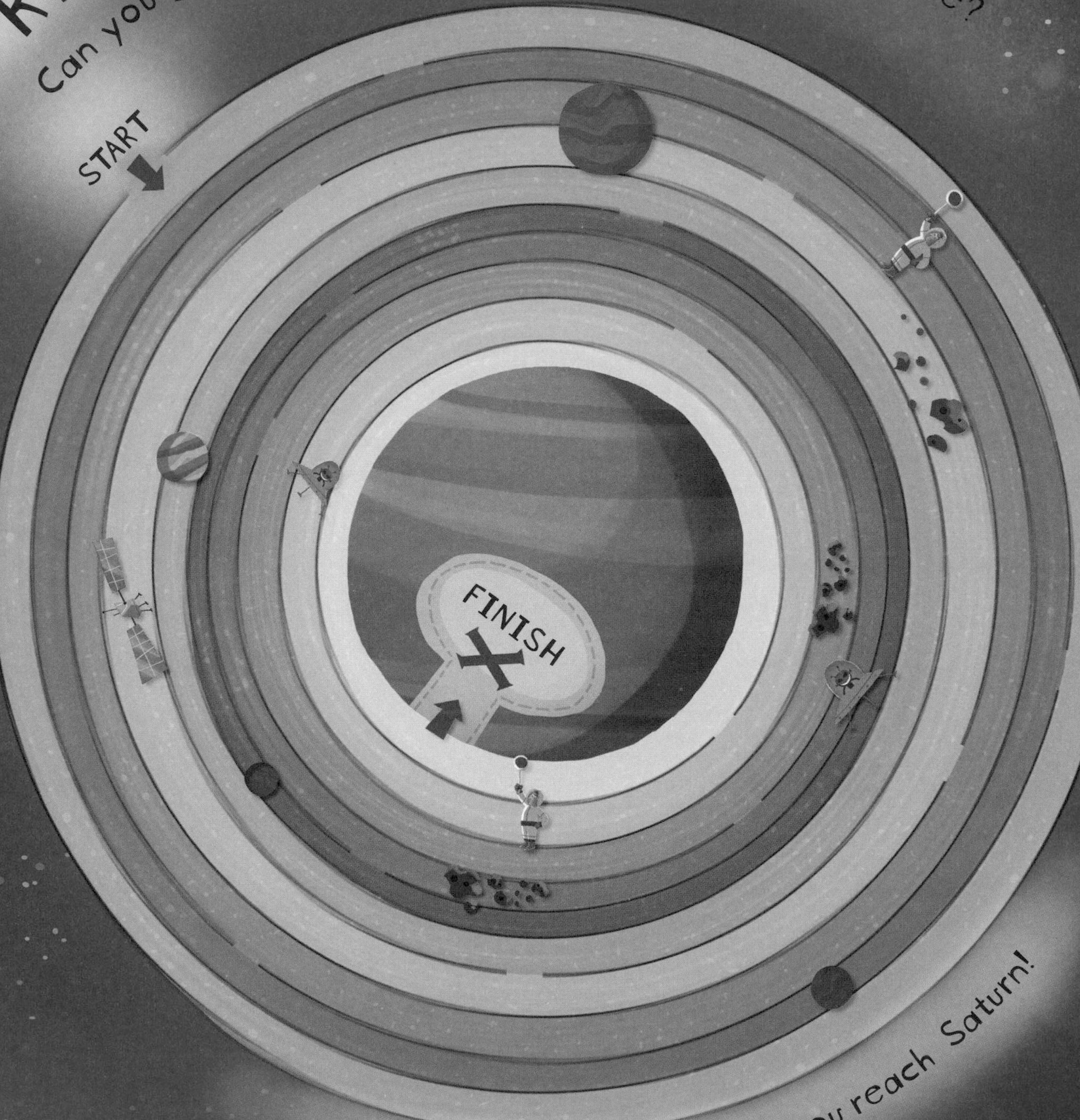

START

FINISH
X

Hop from ring to ring until you reach Saturn!

Turn to page 80 for the answer.

The planet Saturn is mostly made of gas. Saturn is so light it could float in water — if you could find a pool big enough.

SENDING SIGNALS
Earth calling other planets!

Dear Aliens from Outer Space,

Write a message welcoming aliens who want to visit Earth.

_____

_____

_____

_____

If you come to visit our planet Earth, this is what you will see.

Draw your picture here.

LOOKING FOR LIFE

The space probes Voyager 1 and 2, launched in 1977, carry this special gold disc as a message for aliens. The record includes greetings in 55 languages, music, pictures of people, animals and places, plus a star map to our planet. The probes are still travelling in space and are now approaching the edge of our solar system.

GALAXY GAZETTE

Draw yourself here.

Read all about the galaxy's top stories and draw pictures to go with them.

ALIEN PET EATS OWNER

Mrs Jean Ritter of Leeds did not read the warning that came with her pet Carnipod and tried to feed it cat food.

SATURN STAR

The solar system's youngest astronaut has now reached Saturn.

METEOR DANGER!

Astronomers say a one-mile wide meteor will pass very close to Earth next week. Let's hope it misses us!

CAN WE HAVE OUR BALL BACK?

The Mars vs Moon football final was cancelled yesterday when the ball was kicked out of orbit.

METEORITE BITES

Bake these mouth-watering space snacks
to share with your starship crew.

INGREDIENTS

225g self-raising flour

1 tsp baking powder

110g butter

55g brown sugar

1 tsp mixed spice

160g mixed dried fruit
and raisins

1 egg

1 tbsp milk

icing sugar

DIRECTIONS

1. In a bowl, mix together the flour, baking powder and butter until it's crumbly. Then add the sugar, spice and dried fruit.

2. Beat the egg in a cup, then stir it into the mix, with the milk, to make a soft dough.

3. Scoop out tablespoons of the mix, mould them into lumpy meteorite shapes and place them on a baking tray.

4. Sprinkle a little icing sugar on top for stardust, then ask a grown-up to bake them in an oven at 200°C for 15 minutes until golden. Leave them to cool before eating.

STATION GAMMA ALPHA

At Red Giant 572A people live on a giant space station orbiting a massive star.

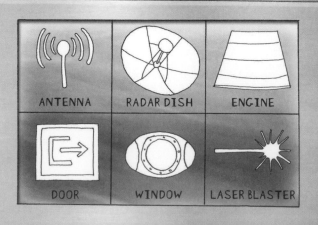

Finish off this space station by drawing the parts shown, or make up your own.

Stars, including our own Sun, are massive balls of super-hot gas that give off the light and heat we need to survive. The Sun is over a million times bigger than Earth, but there are stars in space that are a thousand times bigger than the Sun!

ANTENNA

RADAR DISH

ENGINE

DOOR

WINDOW

LASER BLASTER

ALIEN MASK

Cut out this alien mask to wear at fancy-dress parties across the galaxy.

1. Carefully cut out the mask and eyeholes, following the dotted lines.

2. Cover the holes marked at each side of the mask with sticky tape to reinforce them.

3. Push a pencil through the marked holes.

4. Thread string or elastic through the holes and knot it in place, so that the mask fits snugly on your head.

GALAXY GAGS

Colour in the scenes and fill in the word balloons to create your own jokes.

A WORLD OF YOUR OWN

This moon around Neptune has never been mapped.
Give names to all the mountains, valleys and craters.

CAN YOU ALSO WRITE IN
THE GRID LOCATIONS?

(The first one has been done for you.)

1. Ridge in grid square   ...E./...1...   4. Volcano in grid square   ....../....

2. Valley in grid square   ....../......   5. Ice Cap in grid square   ....../....

3. Crater in grid square   ....../......   6. Mountain in grid square   ....../....

Turn to page 80 for the answer.

STARTER

DRINK

MAIN

DESSERT

ASTRONIBBLES

Space food can be rather dull.
See if you can dream up something more
interesting for you and your crew.

In the early days of spaceflight, astronauts slurped up their dinner in liquid or paste form. Now most of the food taken into space is dried and put into plastic packets, to make it long-lasting and easy to store. Before eating, astronauts have to add water to their dinner.

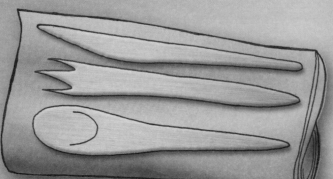

MY FIRST ROCKET

SPACE SNAPS

Ray is telling stories about his time as an astronaut (again). But some of his photos are starting to fade.

Help Ray by colouring them in.

TRAINING

TRUCKING ON THE MOON

MISSION LAUNCH

MY FIRST SPACE WALK

MARS 1 CREW

LIFE ON MARS?

BLAST OFF!

In 1957, the Soviet Union launched a rocket that carried the world's first artificial satellite, Sputnik 1, into space.

Draw a rocket on the launchpad and colour it in.

ZOOM TO THE STARS FLICK BOOK

Make your own flick book and watch your rocket blast off into space.
Turn the page to find out how.

HOW TO MAKE YOUR FLICK BOOK

1. Cut out all the pages of the flip book.

2. Put the pages in the correct order, from page 1 (on top) through to page 32.

3. Ask a grown-up to help you staple the pages together.

4. Hold the book in your left hand, then flip the pages with your right thumb to watch the rocket take off!

4	3	2	1
8	7	6	5
12	11	10	9
16	15	14	13
20	19	18	17
24	23	22	21
28	27	26	25
32	31	30	29

TRUE OR FALSE?

Dip into this Super Space Dictionary. Tick each definition "True" or "False".

ASTEROID
A rock, smaller than a planet, that orbits the Sun. Most asteroids are found between Mars and Jupiter.

True   False

BLACK HOLE
An area of space where gravity is so strong even light can't escape its pull.

True   False

COMET
An icy object travelling through space, leaving a trail of gas and dust behind it.

True   False

GALAXY
A collection of billions of stars, planets, dust and gas.

True   False

GIBBULON
A giant space monkey at the centre of our galaxy.

True   False

LIGHT-YEAR
The distance that light travels through space in one year – 5,878 billion miles.

True   False

MILKY WAY
The name of our galaxy.

True   False

MOON
A world that orbits a planet, such as Earth's Moon.

True   False

OBLONGON
A rectangular planet that orbits the Sun once every five minutes.

True   False

SOLAR SYSTEM
A star and the planets and objects that move around it.

True   False

STAR
A large ball of super-heated gas in space. The Sun is our nearest star.

True   False

SUPERNOVA
An exploding star.

True   False

VORPAL DRIVE
An experimental rocket engine that uses brainwaves to travel through space.

True   False

Turn to page 80 for the answers!

What does the Earth spin around?

What goes around the Earth?

Find a sticker of a comet.

On which planet would you find a storm called the Red Spot?

Find a sticker of the constellation Orion.

SUPER SPACE STICKER QUIZ

Use the stickers at the back of the book to answer this super space quiz.

Which NASA robot landed on Mars in 2012?

What was the first living creature to be sent into space — in 1957?

Which mission was the first to land men on the moon?

64

Turn to page 80 for the answer.

HELLO, HUMANS!

A message has been received from an alien life form.
Use the galaxy decoder to work out what
they are trying to say.

____ _____, __ ___ _____

_ _____ __ ____ ____

_____. __ ___ ___ __

__, ___ ____ ___ _____

_____ _____?

Turn to page 80 for the answer.

GALAXY DECODER

A	B	C	D	E	F	G	H	I	J	K	L	M

N	O	P	Q	R	S	T	U	V	W	X	Y	Z

SPACE LOG

Fill in the details of your space adventure in this journal, then add some drawings and stickers to go with it.

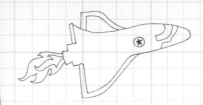 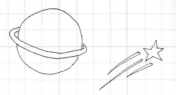

Ready for take-off! ....
....
....

Three days later we were on the Moon ....
....
....

....

There was a lot happening at Mars base ....
....
....
....

....

We were under attack! ....

....

....

....

Our robot needed repairs ....

....

....

I got to meet my first alien, and new best friend ....

....

....

It was the furthest from Earth I have ever been ....

....

....

....

....

....

ALIEN LINE-UP

Aliens from the planet Znuck are all very similar.
Can you spot one small difference in aliens
2 to 9 when compared to alien 1?

The first
one is done
for you.

Turn to page 80 for the answer.

COMET TAILS

Astronaut Alice and her robot helper Evac-28 are investigating a comet.

Comets are icy bodies that orbit the Sun. They have tails of gas and water that point away from the Sun as they move around our solar system.

Spot nine differences in picture 2 compared to picture 1.

Turn to page 80 for the answer.

ROCKET PLAQUE

Make your own shiny plaque to commemorate your space adventure.

WHAT YOU NEED

Pencil
Scissors
Cardboard
Card
Aluminium foil
Black paint and brush

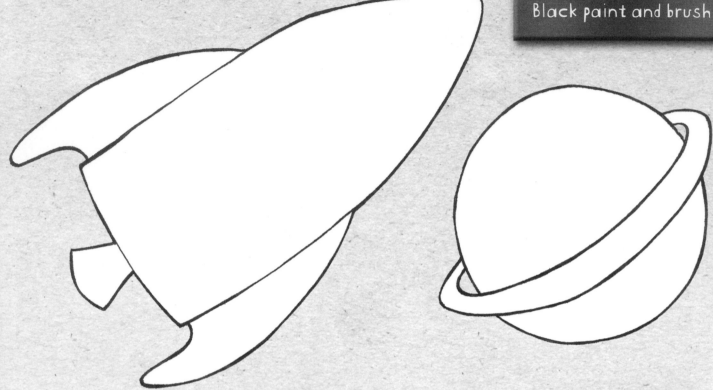

1. Copy the outline of the spaceship and planet onto cardboard.

2. Cut them out and stick them onto a new square of card. Add a cardboard frame.

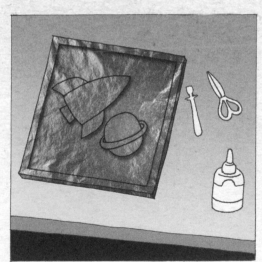

3. Glue foil over the top of the whole picture and rub it down to show the shapes underneath.

4. Use black paint to fill in the space between the shapes and frame. Let it dry then hang it up in your spaceship or bedroom.

BLACK HOLE BEWARE!

RED ALERT! Your spaceship has only just avoided getting sucked into a black hole. Use your stickers to show rockets, planets, rocks and satellites being dragged towards it.

A black hole is an area in space with very strong gravity. It sucks in everything around it, including light! Scientists believe there is one at the centre of our galaxy.

Cut out and send these cards to your friends and let them wonder where you've been!

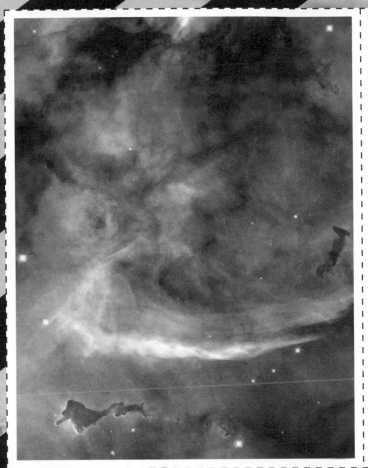

THE CARINA NEBULA - WHAT A VIEW!

ON A SPACEWALK - HI MUM!

LUNAR OBSERVATORY, MOON, 2050

BLAST OFF!

FRIENDLY FACE

A space probe has received a picture from the edge of the galaxy. Follow the guide to colour in the grid squares and reveal the secret picture.

Colour these in black:

ROW A: 6, 7, 8, 9, 15, 16, 17, 18
ROW C: 6, 8, 10, 12, 14, 16, 18
ROW E: 12
ROW F: 11, 12
ROW G: 1, 2, 22, 23
ROW H: 2, 22
ROW I: 1, 2, 6, 8, 10, 12, 14, 16, 18, 22, 23
ROW M: 8, 10, 12, 14, 16
ROW P: 8, 9, 10, 11, 12, 13, 14, 15, 16

Colour these in yellow:

ROW C: 7, 9, 11, 13, 15, 17
ROW I: 7, 9, 11, 13, 15, 17
ROW K: 6, 7, 17, 18,
ROW L: 6, 8, 9, 10, 11, 12, 13, 14, 15, 16, 18
ROW M: 6, 18
ROW N: 6, 8, 9, 10, 11, 12, 13, 14, 15, 16, 18
ROW O: 6, 18
ROW P: 7, 17

Colour these in green:

ROW B: 5, 6, 7, 8, 9, 10, 11, 12, 13, 14, 15, 16, 17, 18, 19
ROW C: 4, 5, 19, 20
ROW D: 4, 5, 19, 20
ROW E: 4, 5, 10, 11, 12, 13, 14, 19, 20
ROW F: 4, 5, 10, 13, 14, 19, 20
ROW F: 1, 2, 4, 5, 10, 13, 14, 19, 20, 22, 23
ROW G: 3, 4, 5, 10, 11, 12, 13, 14, 19, 20, 21
ROW H: 3, 4, 5, 19, 20, 21
ROW I: 3, 4, 5, 19, 20, 21
ROW J: 1, 2, 4, 5, 6, 7, 8, 9, 10, 11, 12, 13, 14, 15, 16, 17, 18, 19, 20, 22, 23
ROW K: 4, 5, 8, 9, 10, 11, 12, 13, 14, 15, 16, 19, 20
ROW L: 4, 5, 7, 17, 19, 20
ROW M: 4, 5, 7, 17, 19, 20
ROW N: 4, 5, 7, 17, 19, 20,
ROW O: 4, 5, 7, 8, 9, 10, 11, 12, 13, 14, 15, 16, 17, 19, 20
ROW P: 4, 5, 6, 18, 19, 20
ROW Q: 5, 6, 7, 8, 9, 10, 11, 12, 13, 14, 15, 16, 17, 18, 19
ROW R: 10, 11, 12, 13, 14

	1	2	3	4	5	6	7	8	9	10	11	12	13	14	15	16	17	18	19	20	21	22	23	
A																								A
B																								B
C																								C
D																								D
E																								E
F																								F
G																								G
H																								H
I																								I
J																								J
K																								K
L																								L
M																								M
N																								N
O																								O
P																								P
Q																								Q
R																								R
	1	2	3	4	5	6	7	8	9	10	11	12	13	14	15	16	17	18	19	20	21	22	23	

Turn to page 80 for the answer.

NEW EARTH

Well done! You've discovered a planet similar to Earth outside our solar system. Use your stickers and colouring pens to complete this picture of New Earth with a space base, astronauts, animals and gardens.

FIVE REASONS WHY I'M THE PERFECT ASTRONAUT

Now you've almost come to the end of your first space mission, tell the Astro Agency why they should send you on more adventures.

TRAINING

I learnt how to _____
_____
_____

BEHAVIOUR ABOARD SPACESHIP

On the spaceship I _____
_____
_____

PLANET EXPLORATION

On other planets I found _____
_____
_____

SPACE BATTLES

In a battle with space pirates I _____
_____
_____

MEETING ALIENS

When I met aliens I _____
_____
_____

Congratulations! You've made it through astronaut school and safely to the edge of our galaxy! Fill in your certificate and hang it in your spaceship cockpit.

THE **A**STRO **A**GENCY

AWARDS

TOP HONOURS

FOR

EXCELLENCE IN
SPACE EXPLORATION

BY ORDER OF

Commander Sam Astro

THE SPACE CREATIVITY BOOK ANSWERS

9

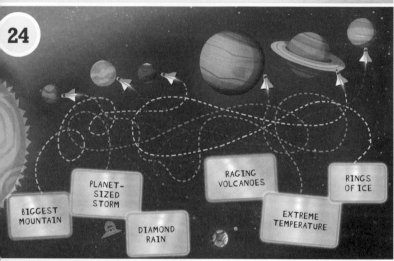

WHERE ARE YOU NOW?

WHOPPA

16

24

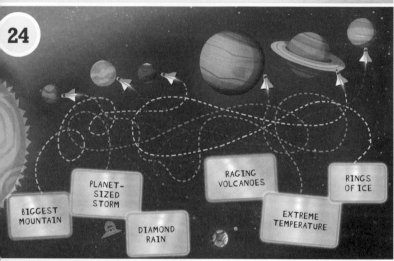

36

40

A K   B U C S
D Q   E G   F N
H O   I R
J M   L T

Odd one out

P

48

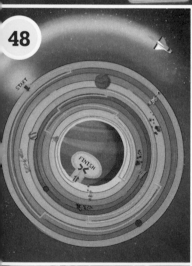

56

1. Ridge in grid square   E / 1
2. Valley in grid square   D / 3
3. Crater in grid square   B / 4
4. Volcano in grid square   F / 4
5. Ice Cap in grid square   D / 7
6. Mountain in grid square   H / 5

63

ASTEROID - True
BLACK HOLE - True
COMET - True
GALAXY - True
GIBBULON - False
LIGHT-YEAR - True
MILKY WAY - True
MOON - True
OBLONGON - False
SOLAR SYSTEM - True
STAR - True
SUPERNOVA - True
VORPAL DRIVE - False

64

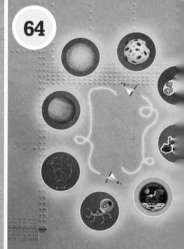

65

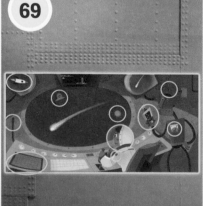

DEAR HUMANS, WE ARE PLANNING A HOLIDAY ON EARTH THIS SUMMER. DO YOU HAVE ROOM FOR ME, MY WIFE AND EIGHT BILLION CHILDREN?

68

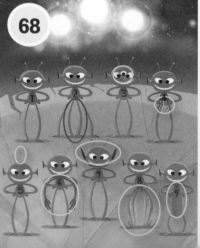

69

75